Flamingos, Poodle Skirts
& Red Hots

Creative Theme Party Ideas

Gloria Hander Lyons

Blue Sage Press

Flamingos, Poodle Skirts & Red Hots
Creative Theme Party Ideas

Inquires should be addressed to:
Blue Sage Press
48 Borondo Pines
La Marque, TX 77568
www.BlueSagePress.com

ISBN: 978-0-9802244-5-0

Library of Congress Control Number: 2008910344

First Edition: November, 2008

Printed in the United States of America

Table of Contents

Flamingos, Poodle Skirts and Red Hots:

Creative Theme Party Ideas

Whether you're planning a traditional feast in the dining room, a candlelit terrace party or a backyard barbecue, any event can be memorable when put together with flair. Turning your event into a theme party can add extra fun and excitement for both you and your guests.

In addition to good food and conversation, unique decorations and fun activities that coordinate with your theme can make an occasion even more special. A little planning and creativity is all it takes to make your event stand out from the rest.

Choosing a theme can be as fun as having the party. The options, of course, are endless, but you'll need to choose a theme that is appropriate for your party, depending on the purpose of the event, the age and number of guests and where and when the event will be held.

Having a theme makes the party planning easier, and enables the guests to be more interactive, especially when asked to wear a costume, a hat or a specific color.

Your theme can be based on a color ("pretty in pink" or "red hot mama's"), a shape (polka dots or stars and stripes), a flower (roses or sunflowers), a food (chocolate or beer), a place (seaside, garden or French bistro), a historical period (Southern Plantation or Roaring Twenties), a holiday or season (winter wonderland or summer picnic).

To plan your party, make a list of every item, food, color, person, place, costume, song, book, project, activity or fact that fits even remotely into your theme. You might need to do a little research for historical periods or foreign countries, but it will make your theme more authentic.

This list will be your guide for choosing the invitations, colors, decorations, food, music and activities for your event.

A fun theme combined with your own personal style will produce a party that is sure to be a hit with your guests, so let your creativity and imagination run wild.

This book offers a simple step-by-step guide for successful party planning, plus a variety of party ideas based on period themes, travel locations, movie or book themes, surprise parties and more. Delight your guests with a 1920's Speak-Easy, a Sizzling Red Hot Birthday, a Sunset Caribbean Caper or a "Mad-Hatter" Bridal Shower.

Also included are clever ideas for invitations, decorations, party favors, food displays and fun activities for your guests.

You'll be the hostess with the most creative ideas. So, what are you waiting for? Pick a theme and let the fun begin!

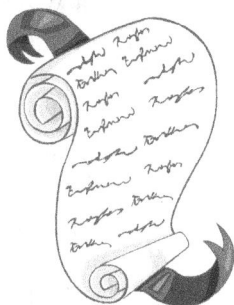

Who's on the Guest List?

After choosing a theme, it's time to start planning your event, and you can't have a party without the guests.

The purpose for your party should determine who will be on your guest list. Is it a birthday party for a family member or a retirement party for a co-worker? Is it for males or females only, or both? Is it for children or adults? Is it for family only, friends only, neighbors only, co-workers only—or a mixture of all of the above?

One main consideration for determining who is on your guest list is that you have adequate space for the number of people you plan to invite. Don't invite more people than you can comfortably accommodate in your home or the facility you plan to use for your event.

For smaller, more intimate gatherings such as a dinner party, consider your guests' personalities and whether they will blend harmoniously or clash violently. You don't want the fun to be over before the party begins, so make sure to invite people who will enjoy each other's company.

For larger groups, try to include people who have a wide variety of interests rather than those whose only common interest is their work.

Try to pique your guests' interest in mingling by posting a sign inside the entrance to your party room that will give them a few clues about the other guests. It might say: "At this party there is one photographer, one surfer, one dog groomer and two mountain climbers. Can you find out who they are?"

Pay careful attention to the personalities, ages, physical abilities and interests of the people you include on your guest list to ensure that everyone will enjoy the festivities.

Getting the Word Out

Now that you've decided on a party theme and made your guest list, you need send out invitations. Create invitations that match your theme and let your guests know what kind of party they'll be attending. A unique invitation will help create anticipation for your event.

Double check your guest list before sending out your invitations to make sure you haven't left anyone out.

Include the following information on the invitation:

- Date (and day)
- Time (starting and ending)
- Place (include directions or a map)
- Occasion (birthday, retirement or shower)
- Party details ("It's a surprise!" or "The shower has a kitchen theme.")
- Attire (black tie, casual or costumes)
- R.S.V.P. phone number

If your party is very formal or requires costumes, send out your invitations three to four weeks before the event. If it's more casual, two weeks in advance is fine.

Keep in mind that your invitation will set the tone for your party. So get creative!

Invitations don't have to be printed on a flat piece of paper. You can send your party details on a balloon, paper fan, ticket, postcard, napkin, travel brochure, baseball card, party hat, wine label, puzzle or a package of vegetable seeds—whatever fits your theme.

A few ideas for creative invitations are listed below:

- For a New Year's Eve party, write the party information on a plastic champagne glass using a silver or gold metallic paint pen. Tie a bow around the base using silver or gold ribbon. Mail the invitations in a box filled with colorful tissue and paper party streamers.

- Old 45 rpm records can set the stage for a fifties or sixties theme dance party. Cut out circles from heavy paper on which to write your party details. Glue the circles to the center of the record using a glue stick. Mail the invitation in a padded envelope. Or cut record shapes from black poster board and add your invitation information on a center label.

- A balloon invitation sets the tone for any festive occasion. Print the party information on a small piece of paper, roll it up tightly and tie with narrow curly ribbon. Place the paper inside a large colorful latex balloon, inflate the balloon with either helium or air, tie the opening closed and add a ribbon bow. Hand deliver your invitations.

- For a fall-theme party, write the party information directly onto a small pumpkin using a permanent marker. Hand-deliver the pumpkin invitations.

- For a Christmas party, write the party information inside a Christmas card and slip it into a small, inexpensive Christmas stocking. Mail in a padded envelope.

- For a baby shower, cut out the shape of a T-shirt from white paper, which is folded in half at the shoulders of the T-shirt. Write the party details inside and slip the T-shirt into a triangle piece of colored paper (blue or pink) that has been folded to look like a diaper and closed with a diaper pin. Mail in a padded envelope.

- For a tropical paradise party, write your party information on a piece of bright colored paper and slip it inside a large sea shell. Hand deliver or mail in a box that is lined with colorful tissue paper.

  For a really unique tropical party invitation, purchase plastic pink flamingoes and hang the invitation around each bird's neck. Plant the birds in your guests' yards during a late-night, clandestine run.

- For a child's birthday party, cut a piece of heavy paper and fold it in half. Apply finger paint to the child's hand (a different color for each finger and palm) and let the child press a handprint onto the front of the invitation. Write the party details inside. (Size the invitation to fit your envelope.)

- For a beach theme party, purchase small, clear plastic bottles with corks from a craft store. Print the party information on a piece of parchment paper, roll it up and tuck inside the bottle. Add a bit of sand to the bottle before sealing it with the cork. Mail in a tissue-lined box.

- For a 4th of July party, write the details for the party on a piece of paper and put it inside a party cracker. To make a cracker, cut a 5" square of poster board, roll it into a tube, overlapping the ends 1/4" and tape together. Wrap with red, white and blue wrapping paper, which extends at least 3" beyond the ends of the tube. Insert the invitation, gather and tie each end of the wrapping paper with ribbon, close to the ends of the tube. Mail in a box.

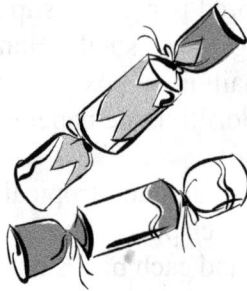

Let your imagination run wild when making your party invitations because this is where the party fun begins for you and your guests.

Planning the Menu

Unless your budget includes the cost of a fancy caterer, keep the party food simple. You don't want to be exhausted by the time your guests arrive. Try to finish as much of the food preparation as you can ahead of time so you won't miss the fun at your own party.

When planning the menu, be sure the food reflects your theme. Whether it's a Mexican Fiesta or a Roman Toga party, you will add more pizzazz to your event if you stick to your theme. So conduct a bit of research to find authentic recipes to offer your guests and practice with a few trial runs before the big day arrives.

Finger foods are easy to make, and they work well for large, stand-up parties. You can also try a serve-yourself salad bar, a dessert contest or a make-your-own-mini-pizza party. Other possibilities for buffet bars might be: a potato bar, pasta bar, fondue bar, crepes bar, pancake bar, taco bar, ice cream sundae bar or burger or sandwich bar.

Whatever food you decide to make for your party, be sure that it is a recipe that you've tried before. Don't prepare a new recipe for your event that you haven't tested—it might not turn out the way you expect.

If you don't like to cook, check out the frozen food section of your local supermarket. There are many choices available for heat and serve appetizers.

How much food should you prepare? That will depend on the type of party: a tea party, a tail-gating party or formal sit-down dinner. It also depends on the appetites of your particular guests. Are they teenage football players or members of the ladies' garden club? You'll need to make your best guess based on these facts.

After estimating the amount of food for the guests who'll be attending your party, it's generally best to make a bit more food than you think you'll need. You can always freeze the leftovers for later use.

Offer a variety of food items for your guests to make sure that everyone will have plenty of food they can enjoy.

A Feast for the Eyes

The food you serve at your party should not only taste good, it needs to look quite festive. You want to amaze your guests with your hosting flair.

The party menu will be more appealing when served on elegant or unusual platters and serving pieces. Keep your party theme in mind when choosing the serving dishes for your food.

For example, use wicker baskets for "An Old Fashioned Picnic" party, hat boxes for a "Mad-Hatter" bridal shower, terracotta pots for a garden party, old-fashioned tins for a kitchen shower or large sea shells for a tropical island party.

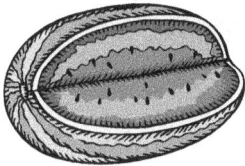

Fruits and vegetables make interesting serving dishes. Scoop out the inside of a watermelon, cantaloupe, orange, pumpkin or bell pepper to form a bowl and place the food inside.

You can also use pita pockets, hollowed out bread loaves and tortillas formed into the shape of a bowl to hold food.

Another fun touch is to give each dish a name that is appropriate to the theme of your party and make a decorative label to display with it.

You might have "Death by Chocolate Brownies" for a Murder Mystery party, or "Yellow Brick Road Butterscotch Bars" for a Wizard of Oz party.

When deciding where to display your party food, don't limit your serving areas to tables—consider using carts, coffee tables, stools and unusual pieces of furniture. Or try theme-related items, such as an ironing board for a wedding shower or luggage for a bon voyage party.

Cover your tables with decorative tablecloths—or make your own by using lengths of colorful print fabric that matches your party theme.

Arrange trays of food on fabric-covered risers (sturdy boxes or pots turned upside down) at different heights to create interest in the display on your buffet table.

You'll find more fun ideas for decorating your buffet table on page 13.

If you want to impress your guests, take the time to ensure that the food for your party is a feast for the eyes, as well as the palate.

Table Decoration Ideas

Your buffet table or dining table will be the focal point for your party, so make sure it dazzles your guests. Start with a tablecloth that fits your theme, then build up from there.

For a buffet table, arrange your serving trays and dishes on risers at various heights to create more interest. You can use sturdy boxes or large pots turned upside down. Cover these with another table cloth or fabric that matches your theme.

For more pizzazz, add flowers, fall leaves, Christmas ornaments, greenery, pumpkins or any other items you can find to reinforce the party theme .

For a seated dinner party, start with a tablecloth that matches your theme, then add an attractive centerpiece, like an arrangement of flowers, fall gourds or Christmas garlands decorated with candles or ornaments. Be sure to keep the centerpiece arrangement low enough so that guests can see over the top.

Add to the table decorations with original placemats you create from items such as paper fans, maps, large photos, mirrors, small straw mats, palm leaves or inexpensive art reproductions.

Napkin Rings

Tuck napkins into napkin rings that match your theme. A few ideas are listed below:

- Use miniature grapevine wreaths decorated with silk flowers that coordinate with the party theme.
- Tie a length of colorful wired–edge ribbon into a bow around a napkin.
- Wrap silk ivy around a napkin for a garden party.
- Use small cookie cutters in the shape of stars, gingerbread men or reindeer for a Christmas dinner.
- Use a pacifier at a baby shower.
- Use a luggage tag at a bon voyage party.
- Wrap eating utensils in a bandana napkin for a Western party.

Place Cards

If you're hosting a sit-down dinner party, use place cards to assign each guest a reserved seat for dining. This will help relieve their anxiety over where they should sit. Place cards that match your party theme will also help decorate the dining table.

You can personalize your guests' party favors and they can do double duty as place cards, such as a Christmas ornament or small picture frame.

A few ideas for place cards are listed on page 15.

- Small framed photographs of family members or friends (especially childhood photos) can serve as place cards and inspire stimulating conversation as well. Give as favors at the end of the party.

- Write each guest's name using a gold or silver paint pen on a Christmas ball ornament. Set the ornament in an artificial evergreen candle ring beside the guest's plate.

- For a child's birthday party, use a paint pen to write each child's name on a small, brightly colored plastic pail and fill with small toys and treats. Set beside each child's place. Give as party favors.

- Use black eye masks for a Halloween party or green or purple masks for a Mardi Gras theme and write the guests' names on them using a paint pen. Embellish each mask with glitter or feathers.

- Party crackers also make great place cards and favors. To make a cracker, cut a 5" square of poster board, roll it into a tube, overlapping the ends 1/4" and tape together. Wrap it with colorful wrapping paper with the ends extending at least 3" beyond the tube on each end. Gather the wrapping paper close to one end of the tube and tie with ribbon to secure. Fill the tube with individually wrapped candy then gather the wrapping paper at the open end and tie with ribbon. Write the guest's name on the cracker and place on the table

More Table Decoration Ideas

- Use gift-wrapped boxes in various sizes as risers to create a tiered table setting for a buffet at a Christmas party or birthday party. A wrapped box, with the lid set aside, can hold rolled napkins tied with ribbons.

- Strings of miniature lights or votive candles add a warm glow to any table setting. Sprinkle them around your buffet table.

- Add a wreath, greenery or flowers (silk or real) around the base of the punch bowl. A string of miniature lights will also add sparkle.

- Lay squares of mirror down the center of your table and place a group of pillar candles on top.

- For a child's birthday party, paint a terracotta pot with bright colors and designs. Fill the pot with Styrofoam and cover with Easter grass. Then insert large, colorful lollipops, which can also be the party favors.

- For a beach theme, fill tall hurricane vases with water and goldfish. Surround the bases with sand and seashells. Use lots of aqua and teal in your decorating scheme to evoke the feeling of the ocean.

- For a Victorian theme, use a white wire birdcage (found at craft centers or import stores) topped with colorful silk flowers, strings of pearls and ribbon. Collect tea cup and saucer sets from garage sales or flea markets as favors for guests. Put a tea light inside each one and place them on your table.

Name Tags

Name tags are a good idea for large parties where many of the guests have never met. Your guests will be impressed when they arrive to find their custom designed name tag waiting for them.

Whether your party is a personal or business-related event, wearing clearly printed name tags will help your guests interact more freely with your friends, family or co-workers when meeting for the first time.

Name tags can also add to the party décor when decorated to match your party theme.

Before the party begins, write your guests' names on the tags in large block letters, using waterproof ink or print them out on your computer. It's best not to let guests write their own tags.

Make sure the tags are safe for fine fabrics. Don't spoil the fun by snagging the fabric on a guest's expensive new outfit.

If an official greeter is assigned to hand out the name tags as your guests arrive, they will be more likely to wear them.

Name tags don't have to be printed on flat pieces of paper. You can make your own custom tags to coordinate with your party theme from supplies such as ribbons, flowers, party buttons, bibs, hats and around-the-neck hang tags.

Use your own creativity to design a unique name tag for your theme party that will surprise and delight your guests. These custom tags can also do double duty as personalized party favors.

A few name tag ideas are listed below:

- Write your guests names on colorful plastic sun visors using a paint pen.
- For a mystery party, cut letters from magazines to spell out each guest's name on a piece of cardboard to look like a ransom note. Hot glue a pin back to the back or thread ribbon through a hole in the top to form a hang tag.
- For a gathering of teachers, purchase mini chalk boards and add each guest's name using a white paint pen. Hot glue a miniature apple to one corner and a pin back or hanging cord to the back.
- For a Valentine's Day party, print each guest's name on an address label and attach to a child's Valentine card. Attach a pin back or hanging ribbon to the back.
- For a Las Vegas/Casino party, print each guest's name on an address label and attach to a playing card. Add a pin back or hanging ribbon to the back.
- For a garden party, hot glue silk flowers to 3" straw hats. Write guests' names on ribbon using a paint pen and attach. Add a pin back or hanging ribbon.
- For a Christmas party, write each guest's name on a tiny Christmas stocking using a glitter pen. Attach a pin back.

Setting the Stage

Whatever theme you choose for your party, you want your guests to feel like they've been transported to another place and time. You can transform your party room into a tropical paradise, a 1920's speak-easy or a Western corral. All it takes is a little imagination and a few props to set the stage.

Refer to your party list for ideas to create just the right atmosphere. To completely immerse your guests in your theme, make sure you touch all their senses: sight, sound, smell, taste and touch.

To set the tone, you might use hay bales as seating for your Western shindig, hire a violinist for your romantic Valentine's Day dinner or turn your living room into a sultan's tent with throw rugs, floor pillows and yards of fabric hanging from the walls for an Arabian Nights theme.

The lighting at your party can dramatically affect the mood. Experiment with dimmer switches, candles, colored light bulbs, paper lanterns, flashlights, Christmas tree lights, tiki torches for outdoor parties, or flashing strobe lights to create the mood you want.

The aroma of fresh evergreen boughs at a Christmas party or sizzling fajitas at your Mexican fiesta will help set the mood for your event. Capitalize on the scents that evoke your theme.

Fill the room with music that is appropriate for your party's theme. Choose classical for a dinner party, rock and pop for a dance party, country for a Western party or eerie sounds for a Halloween bash.

Brainstorm for creative ideas that will transport your guests to another time or place. Set the stage for your festive event with authentic decorations, but don't forget to add appropriate lighting, music and aromas that will completely immerse your guests in your theme.

Make your party an experience that they won't soon forget!

Let the Fun Begin

Choosing fun games and activities for your guests will make your party a hit. Select ones that match your theme, but make sure they are appropriate for your guests' ages and physical abilities.

Plan enough activities to keep the party lively and interesting but be sure to allow time for guests to socialize on their own, as well.

It's always a good idea to award prizes for game or contest winners. Choose prizes that relate to your theme and are appropriate for both men and women, if both sexes are attending your party.

A few party games and activities are listed on the next few pages to help spark your creativity:

- For a New Year's Eve party, ask each guest to come dressed in an outfit that represents a major or minor event that took place in their lives during the year. Half the fun is guessing what event each guest represents. Also, ask your guests to write three New Year's resolutions on a slip of paper. Collect their answers, then read each of them aloud, asking your guests to guess whose resolutions they are.

- For a Christmas party, have a white elephant exchange. Ask each guest to select the worst, most useless gift they have ever received. Have them wrap the item with gift wrap and bring it to your party. Place all the gifts on a display table. Each guest draws a number from one to the number of guests attending the party. The person who draws number one chooses a gift and unwraps it. The person holding number two can either choose a new gift from the table or take the gift that has already been unwrapped. Continue until all the gifts are unwrapped.

- For just about any party theme, you can play a trivia game. Write questions on slips of paper that relate to your party's theme (Christmas, sports, movies, etc.), number them, and tape them around the party room. Provide your guests with pens and paper, and have them write down their answers to the numbered questions. You can write the questions on paper shapes that match your theme—Christmas trees, footballs, ghosts, etc. The decorative shapes will add to the décor of your party room, as well as provide a fun activity. Give a prize to the guest with the most correct answers.

- Entertainment is a good alternative to games. Hire a musician, comedian, magician, graphologist (handwriting analyst), fortune-teller, disc jockey, juggler or local celebrity to entertain your guests. Make sure the entertainment you choose coordinates with your party's theme.

- Your guests can also be your entertainment. Divide them into groups of three or four and have them perform songs or skits that relate to your party theme. For a 1950's party, write the names of popular singing groups on slips of paper, along with the name of a song that group recorded. Have your guests draw numbers to determine what group they will be in and what song they will perform.

Provide the music and words for the song. The group can either lip-sync or sing along with the music. Give the group time to rehearse their "moves" before the performance. Present prizes to each group in a variety of categories: funniest, most creative, most entertaining, etc. This activity can work for just about any party theme.

- If your guests are crafty, have a contest where each guest designs a unique costume or accessory they will wear to your party. One idea is a "Mad Hatter" tea party where each guest wears an outrageous or funny hat that she made herself. Have a fashion show where the guests model their hats on a runway. Award each guest a "prize" for her hat (funniest, most colorful, largest, smallest, most creative, etc.).

Another variation on this theme is a bridal shower "Mad Hatter" party where each guest designs a hat that is covered with small gifts for the bride. See the details on page 53.

- Physical competitions, such as team races, are always a fun party activity if you have the space and your guests are up for the challenge. Try a roping contest at a western party (page 44) or a pancake race at a Shrove Tuesday Party (page 28) with contestants flipping pancakes in a skillet while they run the course. Your guests will have a rousing good time.

- Play a memory game. Divide guests into two groups, with guests sitting side-by-side in each group. Place 10-12 small items that relate to your party theme (like baby items for a baby shower) into two separate brown paper bags. Tell your guests this will be a race to see how quickly they can transfer the items from the bag, pass each one down the line of guests and place them into another paper bag at the end of the line. After all the items have been transferred into the second bag, give each guest a pen and paper and ask them to write down as many items as they can remember that were in the bag. Award a prize to the guest with the most correct answers.

- Make up your own board game, such as Bingo, with topics that relate to your party's theme. Draw a grid on a piece of paper that has four columns with five squares in each column. Make a copy for each of your guests. Think of at least 25 words that relate to your theme. Write them on a sheet of paper and make multiple copies. Cut out the words and paste them into the squares on each Bingo card. You'll need one for each guest. Place the words in different squares on each card and vary the words used. Give each guest a colored marker and ask them to mark off the words as they are drawn from a bowl and called out.

- Scavenger hunts are always fun. Place items around your house or yard before the party begins. Then give each guest or team of guests a map with clues and see who can find the most items first.

- If your space is limited, have a "sit-down" scavenger hunt. This is a fun game to play during a wedding shower, baby shower or tea party. Ask each guest to search her purse for a list of items, such as a brush, a ball-point pen, lipstick, blush, a credit card, a safety pin, emery board, rubber band, shopping list, breath mints, nail clippers, pain reliever, a five-dollar bill, a mirror, eye glasses, chewing gum, hand cream, or other items you want to include. Award a prize to the guest with the most items found in her purse.

- Play a "pass the prize" game. Have guests sit in a circle. Hand a small prize (it can be gift wrapped if you like) to one guest. Read a poem or short story that you have written that repeats a word at least ten times during the game. Each time the guests hear the word, they must pass the prize to the guest on their left. The word should relate to your theme, like "chocolate". For extra entertainment, use two gifts which are passed in opposite directions during the game. The guest holding the prize when the story ends is the winner.

- A "word scramble" game is fun. Think of at least ten words that relate to your theme. For example a Fall party might include: pumpkin, autumn, fall leaves, scarecrow, apples, hay bale, thanksgiving, etc. Scramble each word and print the list onto pieces of paper. Give guests a pen and see who can unscramble the words first.

- For a wedding anniversary party, surprise the honorees by re-creating their wedding (or if the couple eloped, creating the wedding they never had), complete with minister, flowers and wedding cake. And don't forget to take lots of photos or video record the event so the couple will have a reminder of their special day.

- Preserve the Memories: Don't pass up an opportunity to photograph your guests at their most ridiculous or ravishing best, wearing costumes or participating in the party activities. Take photos of your guests against a special photo backdrop or take candid action photos during the party activities. Print out your photos and place them in small frames for party favors.

- Video and Watch: For parties with lots of action, like dance contests or modeling shows, you might want to video the activities and show the recording for your guests' entertainment during the last hour of the party.

Theme Party Ideas

Use the some of the theme party suggestions described on the following pages to help plan the festivities at your next event.

Theme Parties Based on Holidays

Valentine's Day Tea Party

Host a crafty Valentine's Day tea party for your female friends.

Your invitation can be written on a hand-crafted Valentine and mailed in a heart-shaped box.

Ask all your guests to wear red or pink. All decorations and as much of the food as possible should be red or pink and/or cut into the shape of hearts.

Serve cranberry tea in pretty teacups and tiny tea sandwiches cut into heart shapes and served on elegant china. Desserts can be heart-shaped petit fours frosted with pink icing and mini cheesecakes topped with cherry pie filling.

Have craft supplies (lace, beads, stickers, markers, colored paper, etc.) on hand so each person can make a Valentine for their sweetheart. Give prizes for the best hand-made Valentine in several categories: most colorful, most ornate, most sentimental, etc.

For favors, give foil-wrapped chocolates bundled in red tulle and tied with satin ribbon.

Shrove Tuesday
Pancake Party

Shrove Tuesday, also known as "Pancake Day" is the last day for celebration and feasting before the period of fasting required during the Lenten season.

For this party, attach your invitation to an inexpensive plastic spatula and mail in a padded envelope.

Serve pancakes with a variety of different toppings, such as fruit, chopped nuts, chocolate chips, whipped cream, jams, and flavored syrups or butters. Add a few choices for sides, such as bacon, sausage and ham. Then let the guests create their own pancake masterpieces.

For a fun activity, have a pancake race. Prepare pancakes ahead of time for this event. Separate guests into two teams. Give each team a small skillet containing one pancake. Each team forms a line. The first contestant in each line holds the skillet with a pancake inside. When the start signal is given, each contestant runs or walks down to a certain point marked by a chair or other object, goes around it and returns to the line to pass off the skillet to the next team member. During their trip, each contestant must flip the pancake into the air and catch it in the pan 3 times. The first team to finish is the winning team. If the pancake is dropped, the contestant must start over. Have extra pancakes on hand to replace any that fall apart during the race.

Be sure to video record the competition. For guest favors, give tiny bottles of maple syrup.

St. Patrick's Day Bash

Whether you're Irish or not, you and your guests can enjoy celebrating this "lucky" day. Write your party details on a plastic beer mug, using a green paint pen. Mail in a box that is lined with green tissue paper. Be sure to ask your guests to wear green.

Cut large shamrocks from poster board to hang from the ceiling and walls of your party room. Paint a rainbow and a pot of gold on a large banner to hang on the wall. Cover your serving table with a green tablecloth. Your centerpiece can be a black pot filled with bags of gold foil-wrapped chocolate coins, which are the guest favors.

Serve drinks from green plastic beer mugs. If you're serving beer, tint it green with food coloring. In honor of the Irish potato, serve a baked potato bar, with lots of toppings: grated cheese, chopped ham, bacon bits, sour cream, butter, onions, cooked broccoli or green peas, etc. For dessert, serve petit fours or sugar cookies cut into the shape of shamrocks and iced with green frosting.

For a fun activity, cut out 10 or 12 small shamrocks from green construction paper. Write an Irish related question on each one and number each question from 1 to 12. Tape the shamrocks on the walls around the party room. Provide paper and pens and ask guests to write down their answers to each question, but give them a limited amount of time, about 5 minutes, depending on the number of guests. The person with the most correct answers when time runs out wins a prize.

Give each guest an instant "scratch-off" lottery ticket and let them reveal their results.

Fourth of July Potluck Party

Have an old fashioned outdoor potluck dinner with country-style decorations and fun outdoor competitions, like sack races and horseshoe pitching.

Coordinate with your guests for the types of dishes they will contribute. Be sure to ask them to bring copies of the recipe to share with your other guests or supply country-themed recipe cards for guests to copy recipes during the party.

Your invitation can be mailed inside a party cracker. See page 8 for instructions. Ask guests to wear patriotic colors.

Cover the serving tables with old quilts or red-checked fabric. Use bouquets of sunflowers in mason jars for centerpieces. Use jars of homemade jam (or purchase jars of jam at the grocery story) as place cards which can also double as party favors. Print the guests' names on adhesive labels and attach to the jars.

Serve the food from wicker picnic baskets lined with gingham or red and white or blue and white homespun fabric. Use mason jars for drinking glasses.

Try a few of the following for fun activities:
- Hold a cake walk
- Have an old fashioned square dance
- Offer a hay ride
- Make homemade ice cream with a hand-cranked ice cream freezer
- Stage a watermelon eating contest

Halloween Murder Mystery Party

Try a murder mystery theme where the guests dress as their favorite detective and the other guests try to guess their identity.

Attach the invitation to a small magnifying glass and mail in a padded envelope.

Set the mood by dimming the lights and using lots of candles. Play spooky music or a sound track of a thunderstorm. Give prizes for the best costume in several categories, funniest, most famous, most mysterious, etc.

For the activity, play a murder mystery game. Each guest, or team of guests, chooses a folded piece of paper with the name of a person who was murdered written on the front (make up a different name for each guest or team) and a message inside that says to look for a particular symbol (knife, rope, candlestick, axe, gun, bottle of poison) to find the murder weapon clue. These clues (also on folded pieces of paper) are taped around the room. Each guest or team will be searching for a different symbol. When they find it, they will open it to find a clue inside that says what the murder weapon was and another symbol that will tell them where the person was murdered (book for library, plant for conservatory, bed for bedroom, car for garage, etc.). Repeat the clue search for who committed the crime, using symbols for names (Pickle, Cherry, Hand, Rose, Glass, etc.) The last clue they find will lead them to their reward, the guest favor(s) inside a bag with the symbol on the front.

Serve food that is labeled with fun names such as "Death by Chocolate Cookies", "Felonious Fudge" or "Who Dunnit Fondue".

Christmas Ornament & Cookie Exchange

Christmas is always a fun time to get together with friends and family, especially when exchanging gifts and food.

Attach an inexpensive, non-breakable Christmas ornament to your invitation with ribbon and mail it in a box that is lined with colorful tissue paper. Ask each guest to bring a gift-wrapped Christmas ornament and 2 dozen cookies in a pretty basket to your party.

Get out all your Christmas decorations to make your party room extra festive. Don't forget to include evergreens for a Holiday scent and Christmas music to set the mood. Add lots of twinkle lights around the room and on serving tables for more sparkle.

Cover two serving tables with green and red tablecloths. One will be the gift table and the other will hold the baskets of cookies that your guests bring. Create risers (sturdy boxes or pans turned upside down and covered with fabric) to raise the baskets at various heights for a more interesting display.

Serve savory appetizers and tea sandwiches in addition to the cookies. Wassail is a good choice for punch because it scents the entire house with Holiday spices.

Play the gift exchange game described on page 22, where each guest draws a number and takes turns opening a gift or takes a gift that someone else has already opened.

Provide Christmas theme bakery boxes for each guest to take home a selection of cookies from the cookie exchange.

Parties Based on Period Themes

Renaissance

The invitation should be written in Old English script on parchment paper, rolled into a scroll and tied with ribbon. Be sure to tell your guests to wear a period costume. Suggestions for costumes: court jester, town crier, peasant farmer, a lord, a merchant, a king or queen, a lady in waiting, a bar maid or gypsy.

Give prizes for the best costumes in several categories: most authentic, most creative, most humorous, etc.

Decorate your party space with tapestries hung on the walls and try creating a family shield cut from cardboard.

Use long wooden tables with benches for guests to sit while helping themselves to huge platters of roast beef, turkey legs, loaves of bread and bite-size veggies and desserts. (No eating utensils allowed.) Drink wine from goblets.

Divide guests into random groups and have them perform typical Renaissance entertainment such as juggling, singing ballads or dancing.

Play recorded medieval period music and hire or enlist talented friends to dress as a gypsy to read palms or act as a roving minstrel playing an instrument.

Take photos of your guests in their costumes in front of a Renaissance themed background (perhaps a painted stone archway in a castle) and place in a small, bejeweled frame to give as favors.

Ancient Greece or Rome

The invitation should be written on parchment paper, rolled into a scroll and tied with ribbon. Mail in a small box or padded envelope. Ask your guests to wear togas (sheets) and sandals, or more elaborate costumes, such as a Roman Emperor, Roman soldier or Greek Goddess, if they prefer.

Give each guest a crown of leaves (made from silk or real branches) to wear during the party.

Award prizes for costumes in several categories.

Serve Greek food, such as dolmas (stuffed grape leaves), souvlaki (cubes of meat grilled on a skewer) and baklava, and drink wine from goblets. Serve food from low tables, such as coffee tables, and provide floor pillows for guests to lounge around the tables while eating.

Play recorded harp music.

For activities, divide your guests into two teams and play a trivia game with questions about Greek and Roman gods. Set up a few "Olympic style" games of competition (simple relay races or shooting targets with a toy bow and arrow). Award prizes to the winners.

Take pictures of your guests in their costumes and place in a small frame for favors.

Roaring Twenties

The 1920's period, also known as the "Roaring Twenties", is a great period to recreate for a party.

Be sure to include on your invitation the "secret password" your guests will need to say in order to gain entrance to a "roaring good time".

The ladies on your guest list should wear "flapper" costumes of short fringed dresses, long pearl necklaces, feather boas, cigarette holders, sequined headbands, fishnet hose and high heels.

The men wear gangster hats, vests, black ties and shirts and/or "zoot" suits and shoulder holsters for hand guns or carry toy Tommy guns.

Create the ambiance of a "speak easy" with a gun check at the door and period jazz music from Duke Ellington and Bessie Smith.

For a fun activity, stage a Charleston dance contest. Award prizes for costumes and dance contest winners in several categories.

Label some of your food offerings with fun names, like "Bootlegger Brownies", Charleston Cherry Cheesecake" or "Prohibition Punch". For the ultimate roaring twenties prop, bathtub gin, fill a small claw-foot tub with ice to hold bottled drinks.

This is a party you'll want to video records and play during the last half hour of the event. Take pictures of couples in their costumes and give as favors in small frames.

1950's Sock Hop

Recreate a malt shop theme for your party guests.

Use old 45 rpm records for your invitations. Cut out a circle from heavy paper on which to write your party details. Glue the circle to the center of the record using a glue stick. Mail the invitation in a padded envelope.

Ask female guests to wear poodle skirts, neck scarves, white socks and loafers. Male guests can wear short sleeved button-up shirts with the sleeves rolled up, jeans, socks and loafers (hair grease is optional).

For fun activities, play a game of "name that tune" with vintage 1950's records then stage a dance contest featuring dances like the Twist, the Mashed Potato and the Swim. Divide guests into two teams and play a trivia game using questions about TV shows from the period, or familiar quotes such as, "Gee, Wally!" from "Leave It to Beaver" or "Oh, Ricky!" from "I Love Lucy," and see if your guests can name the show.

Serve old-fashioned burgers, fries and malts.

Record the action on video and take lots of photos of your guests to give as favors.

Another option for this era is a 1950's prom night theme, complete with yearbook photos for decorations on the walls or tables, or use them for nametags if you can find them for each guest. The ladies wear old prom dresses and wrist corsages. The men sport ruffled-shirts with old fashioned pastel tuxedos. Don't forget to create a romantic backdrop for taking pictures of each couple.

1970's Disco Dance Party

This party is all about dancing to the tunes from the 1970's. Attach your invitation to a disco ball key chain (available on the internet, search for "disco party supplies") and ask guests to dress in period clothing: polyester leisure suits with bell bottoms and heavy gold chains for the men. Polyester "wrap" dresses or bell bottom pants and halter tops for the ladies. Afro wigs, big sunglasses and anything tie-dyed will also work.

Hang a beaded curtain over the entrance to your party room and greet guests with a "jive" hand shake. Hang posters of "Saturday Night Fever", peace signs or yellow smiley faces. Burn incense, using aromas that were popular in the 1970's, like Patchouli.

A dance floor flooded with colored lights and a disco ball hanging from the ceiling are a must. Use a spotlight to make your disco ball sparkle. A strobe light is also a nice touch. Leave the area outside the dance floor fairly dark and punctuate with light from lava lamps or fiber optic lamps. Add a few bean bag chairs if you have them.

Serve fondue from pots with long forks, either cheese fondue and/or chocolate fondue for dessert. Offer finger foods to make it easier to mingle and dance.

Award prizes for a dance contest and costumes in several categories. Stage group dances like the Hustle and Funky Chicken to make sure everyone gets in on the action.

Hand out mood rings or packages of "Pop Rocks" candy for favors (also available on the Internet).

Victorian Christmas Progressive Dinner Party

You can make a regular progressive dinner party more memorable by choosing a unique theme for the food, costumes and transportation, as guests progress from one dinner course and location to the next.

A Victorian Christmas theme is a good choice. Coordinate the event with two or three friends, so the guests will make at least three stops.

Print your formal invitation in elegant script inside an old fashioned Currier and Ives Christmas card. Ask your guests to wear Victorian costumes.

Each location should be decorated with an abundance of Victorian style Christmas trees and decorations.

Arrange for vintage automobiles to transport guests from one location to the next.

The buffet tables or dining tables at each stop are decked out with your finest china, crystal, silverware and linens. Use candelabras to create an elegant mood.

Serve food that was typical of the period, such as standing rib of beef with Yorkshire pudding, roasted goose or turkey, cranberry pie, mince pie and plum pudding.

Gather around a piano or the Christmas tree to sing old-fashioned Christmas carols. For favors, give each guest a Victorian "wonder ball", a tiny gift wrapped in yards and yards of yarn or long, narrow crepe paper strips.

Parties Based on Travel Locations

Bon Voyage Party

For a Bon Voyage party, the all decorations, food and activities are based on the voyager's destination.

Use travel brochures about the destination for your invitation. Print the party information on adhesive labels and attached them to the inside.

Ask guests to dress for the vacation spot—whether it's Germany, Japan, Africa, or Disney World. Or have them dress as tacky tourists, complete with loud shirts, cameras, sunglasses and suitcases.

The food and decorations for your party should be common to the destination spot.

Give prizes for the best tourist costume in several categories: funniest, most unusual, most elaborate, most creative, etc.

If the guest of honor is going to a foreign country, get a traveler's phrase book, and write down some interesting foreign language phrases. Ask everyone to write down their translation of the phrases, and read the answers aloud. You should get some pretty funny answers.

Give travel-related prizes (try to find ones that relate to your destination spot) to the guest with the most correct answers.

A Caribbean Sunset Caper

Write your invitation on hot pink note cards or on ones printed with a flamingo or beach scene. Ask guests to wear their most colorful island attire. Tuck the invitations into a seashell and deliver them in person or mail in a tissue-lined box.

Purchase or make your own pink flamingos from wood to decorate your party space. Add potted plants, wicker furniture, tropical flowers, a hammock, snorkels, flippers, straw bags or even colorful fake fish attached to fish nets hanging on the wall or fence. Use tiki torches if your party is outside or tiny white Christmas lights inside or out for a festive sparkle.

Arrange tropical fruit including bananas, pineapples, coconuts, mangos, etc. for your table centerpiece. Choose bright tropical-prints for the tablecloth and napkins.

Serve island foods like Jerk Chicken, Coconut Shrimp and Mango Salad. Colorful drinks served in coconuts or stemmed glasses with tiny umbrellas are always fun.

Play recordings of calypso music in the background and encourage your guests to dance. Search for barefoot treasure by filling a child's inflatable swimming pool with clean sand. Let your guests search for small trinkets using only their feet.

Play a game of limbo. Each person tries to go under a wooden dowel suspended between two braces. If he falls or touches the ground, he is eliminated from the contest. Lower the dowel for each round until only one person remains. Award a prize to the winner.

Chinese New Year Party

The Chinese New Year is celebrated at the end of January. The traditional colors for this event are red and gold to symbolize happiness and wealth. Place your invitation inside a red Chinese take-out box, along with a fortune cookie and mail in a box that is lined with gold or black tissue paper. Ask your guests to wear red.

Decorate your serving table with a red tablecloth and a floral centerpiece, such as white orchids. Add accents of gold and black in the form of lacquered serving bowls and trays. Serve traditional Chinese food. And don't forget to include fortune cookies. You can purchase these cookies with customized fortunes at specialty food stores or on the Internet.

Play recorded Chinese music to help set the mood. Hang lots of Chinese lanterns from the ceiling and place red votive candles around the room. Tall bamboo plants are also a nice touch.

For a fun activity, stage a dragon parade, using a handmade paper dragon, or buy one from a party supply store. Hand out toy drums and gongs for guests to play while others parade around the room with the paper dragon.

Post the 12 signs of the Chinese Zodiac, along with the qualities that go with each one, and let guests guess which sign they were born under.

For favors, give "lucky red envelopes" with a brand new $1.00 bill inside.

"Around the World" Christmas Party

Host an "Around the World" Christmas party to celebrate the Holiday season through many different cultures.

Your invitation can be attached to a small globe and mailed in a tissue-lined box. Ask your guests to come dressed in costumes from their favorite country.

Write the words "Merry Christmas" in several different languages on large banners to hang on the walls of your party room. Decorate several small buffet tables to represent different countries: Mexico, England, France, Greece, Italy, Germany, Brazil, etc.

Display the country's flag on each table and use decorations, colors and food from the region. Make small signs for each table explaining some of the country's Christmas traditions, decorations and food. Place a tiny Christmas tree on each table, decorated with regional ornaments.

Play a Christmas trivia game where guests write down their answers to questions about Christmas traditions from various countries. Give a prize to the winner.

Divide guests into groups to perform Christmas carols— preferably those from foreign countries. Supply the words and music and let each group rehearse for their performance.

At the end of the party, break a piñata in the Mexican buffet area and share the goodies as favors.

Ancient Egypt Party

Transport your guests back to ancient Egypt, starting with your invitation. Write the party information on a piece of parchment paper. Roll it up and tie with ribbon, then tuck it inside a three-dimensional pyramid shaped box. Mail in a tissue-lined box. Ask guests to wear period costumes: Cleopatra, a mummy, an archaeologist or an Egyptian king or God.

Decorate the room with palm trees, large baskets or pottery and lengths of fabric draped on the walls. Fold heavy paper into large Egyptian-style fans on long poles. Hang posters of desert scenes, pyramids and the Sphinx.

Give each guest a cartouche: a name tag printed with their first name that has been translated into hieroglyphics. You can find hieroglyphic alphabets on the Internet.

Serve pita bread, chunks of chicken or lamb grilled on skewers, grapes, dates, figs, hummus and other Egyptian type foods on large platters. Drink wine from goblets. For a centerpiece, make a cake in the shape of a pyramid.

Award prizes in several categories for costumes. For a fun activity, play the song "Walk Like an Egyptian" and video record guests performing their best Egyptian walk.

For favors, give each guest a pyramid-shaped box filled with gold foil-covered chocolate coins.

Western Dude Ranch Party

Round up all your friends for a boot-scootin' good time. Cut your invitation into the shape of a boot and write your information on the back. Attach to a doll-size cowboy hat and mail in a tissue-lined box. Ask your guests to come dressed in Western gear: denim jeans or skirts, boots, vests, bandanas and hats. Spurs are optional

Stack a few hay bales at the entrance to the party location and include a sign with the name of your ranch. Or use hay bales as part of the seating inside the party room. Add an old saddle or wagon wheel if you can borrow or rent them.

Give each guest a personalized sheriff's badge for favors that also serve as name tags.

Cover your serving tables with red checked tablecloths. Wrap bandana napkins around each set of eating utensils. Use enamelware plates and mugs. Your centerpiece can be a pair of cowboy boots filled with real or silk wildflowers.

Serve barbecue beef or chicken with the usual sides of potato salad, ranch-style beans (in a cast iron Dutch oven) and Cowboy Cookies for dessert. Serve chips or cookies from cowboy hats turned upside down and lined with bandanas.

For fun activities, have a roping contest. Set up a saw horse with a longhorn skull attached (real or plastic). Let guests take turns trying to lasso the steer from a predetermined distance. Play country western music and clear a space for guests to dance. Stage a few line dances to encourage everyone to participate.

Book or Movie Theme Parties

Aladdin's Lamp/Arabian Nights

Create a magical night with an exotic Arabian theme for your guests.

Write the party information on the back of an invitation cut into the shape of a flying carpet or Aladdin's lamp. Ask the men to dress in traditional Arabian costumes, turbans are optional. Belly dancing costumes with lots of scarves are fun for the ladies.

Turn your living room into a sultan's tent by draping yards of colorful fabrics on the walls and scattering throw rugs and floor pillows around the room for lounging. A few tall potted palm trees will help set the mood.

Play music from the soundtrack for "Lawrence of Arabia" or other Middle Eastern style music.

Serve traditional Middle Eastern food, such as falafel, hummus, egg plant dip, almond crescent cookies and baklava, on low tables.

Dim the overhead lights in the room and create a magical ambiance with lots of votive candles.

Award prizes for the best costumes in several categories. For a fun activity, hold a belly dancing contest (for men and women). Be sure to video record this event and show during the last half hour of the party.

Have each guest write three wishes on a piece of paper and place them in a basket. Read them aloud and ask your guests to guess who wrote them.

Gone with the Wind

Your invitation can be a silk Magnolia attached by satin ribbon to a formal invitation announcing "A Ball for the Ladies and Gentlemen of Southern High Society Before the Dreaded War." Mail the invitation in a box lined with green tissue paper.

Ask the ladies to wear Southern belle ball gowns (hoops are optional) and white gloves and carry parasols or fans. The men should wear Rhett Butler-style jackets with tails, white gloves and ascots and carry walking canes. Top hats would be a nice touch.

Present each lady with a small wrist corsage and each gentleman with a boutonniere as they arrive.

The buffet tables should be elegant and covered with crisp white linens, floral centerpieces, and silver candelabras and serving trays. Serve Southern finger food, like fried chicken strips, tiny biscuits filled with baked ham, pecan tarts and Mint Juleps.

If your budget allows, hire a string quartet to play period dance music or play recorded music from the period. Clear an area for a dance floor for waltzing.

Award prizes for the best costumes in several categories and for the couple who performs the best dance.

Divide the group into two teams and play a game of trivia using questions about the movie or Southern traditions.

Treasure Island

Draw a treasure map on parchment paper for your invitation. If you like, roll it up into a scroll and tie with ribbon and mail in a small box.

This party can be held inside or outside on a patio or deck. Decorate the space with a tropical island theme, complete with palm trees and coconuts. And don't forget to include a pirate's flag and a colorful parrot (real or fake).

Ask your guests to dress in pirate costumes and give prizes for the best costume in several categories: scariest, funniest, most authentic, most imaginative etc.

The buffet table centerpiece can be a cardboard box decorated as a treasure chest that is filled with small draw-string bags of foil-wrapped chocolate coins to give as favors.

Serve Caribbean-style food, like Jerk Chicken, Coconut Shrimp and Mango Salad. Drink hot buttered rum from tankards.

For a fun activity, divide the guests into random groups, give each group a map that has clues written on parchment paper and send them off on a hunt for treasure that you have hidden previously.

Have groups of guests perform various pirate songs. Provide the music and words and let them rehearse before their performances. Video record the event and play the video during the last half hour of the party.

Wizard of Oz Party

Cut your invitation from red card stock into the shape of a Ruby slipper and sprinkle it with red glitter. Write the party details on the back and ask guests to dress as their favorite characters from the movie.

Roll out a yellow plastic runner in the entrance to your party space to represent the yellow brick road. Draw rectangular shapes using a permanent marker for bricks.

Hang posters from the movie around the room. Paint or purchase a large banner with a rainbow for a backdrop to photograph your guests in their costumes. Play the soundtrack from the movie during the party.

Cover your serving table with Wizard of Oz print fabric or an emerald green cloth to represent the Emerald City. Serve some of the food from wicker baskets with handles (like the one Dorothy carried in the movie). Serve drinks from ruby red plastic glasses. Label the food with fun names, like "Yellow Brick Road Cookie Bars" and "Over the Rainbow Punch".

For a fun activity, divide the guests into two teams and play a trivia game with questions from the movie. Or stage a witch's broom race with two teams competing in a relay race while riding on brooms through a maze of props.

For a really spectacular event, hire a balloonist to give rides in a hot air balloon. Don't forget the video camera!

Miscellaneous Party Themes

Academy Awards Party

The theme of this party is the glitter and glamour of Hollywood; complete with black tie and evening gowns (don't forget to tell your guests to wear sunglasses).

For the invitations, cut star shapes from poster board, spray with silver metallic paint and glitter, and write your party information on the back.

Roll out a red carpet runner for your guests. Interview each couple as they enter the party, pretending to be famous movie stars (real or imagined). Have someone video record the moment. Play the recording on a large screen television during the party.

For a small group of guests, stage a formal seated dinner using your best china, crystal and silver. For a large group, serve cocktails, hors d'oeuvres and fancy desserts from elegant buffet tables.

Hang silver, glittered star shapes from the ceiling on black and silver streamers. Hang posters of movie stars on the walls—either black and white photos of famous stars of the past or your favorite new stars.

Play a movie trivia game where guests answer questions about popular movies or identify famous lines from award-winning movies.

Take photos of your guests in front of a background covered with glittery stars to give as favors in small rhinestone-studded frames.

A Garden Tea Party

Hold this party outside in a garden or on a porch or patio for a group of ladies.

Attach your invitation to the back of a packet of vegetable seeds and mail in a padded envelope. Ask your guests to wear pretty straw hats.

Decorate the area using rakes, shovels, hoes, watering cans, baskets and clay pots filled with plants, vegetables and fruit. Use a vegetable-print fabric for a tablecloth and napkins and use a large basket filled with colorful vegetables or a watering can filled with flowers for a centerpiece.

Using a paint pen, write each guest's name on a tiny terracotta pot that contains an herb plant. Arrange the pots on your dining tables at each place setting to serve as both place cards and favors.

Serve foods made with fresh herbs and vegetables, like zucchini bread, dainty tea sandwiches made from chicken salad seasoned with fresh dill, cherry tomatoes stuffed with a blend of cream cheese and fresh basil, chocolate mint brownies and chamomile tea served with lemon and honey. Use terra cotta pots, wicker baskets and garden pails for serving containers.

For entertainment, provide pens and paper to each guest and ask them to answer the following question: "If you were a vegetable or flower, what would you be and why?" Gather the responses and read them out loud. See if your guests can guess who wrote each one. Or make up your own version of a garden bingo game (described on page 24) for guests to play.

Sizzling Red Hot Birthday Party

Tired of the usual "over the hill" birthday party? Try a "sizzling red hot" party for your female friends. This is a good example of how to use a color as the theme for a party. Your invitation should announce that the honoree is Forty (Fifty, Sixty) and Red Hot! Invite your guests to join you in celebrating a "sizzling red hot birthday." Ask them to wear red and bring a "red hot" gift that is wrapped in red paper. Mail the invitation in a red box.

Welcome your guests with a festive banner announcing the "Sizzling Red Hot Birthday for _____." Use the wrapped gifts to decorate the center of the dining table. Tie strips of red tulle and gold metallic ribbon around white napkins and set red votive candle holders at each place setting. For place cards, cut red tulle into 5" squares, fill with red hot candies, bring the corners to the center, and secure using narrow red and gold ribbons. Attach a small white card with each guest's name written in gold ink.

Serve as many "red" and "spicy hot" foods as possible, like meatballs in marinara sauce, salsa with red tortilla chips, mini cheesecakes topped with cherry pie filling, and chocolate dipped strawberries.

Opening the red-hot birthday gifts should keep your guests entertained. For another activity, provide each guest with paper and a pen and ask them to list as many phrases as they can in two minutes using the word "hot". (Examples: "hot as a pistol" or "hot tamales") The winner gets a "steamy" prize.

If your guests need gift ideas, you might suggest a romance novel, red lingerie or gift certificate for a manicure, pedicure or massage.

Spanish Tango Party

This party combines elegance with the passion of the Tango. For the invitation, write the party details on white paper. Roll up like a scroll. Tie with black ribbon and tuck a red silk rose under the ribbon. Mail in a white box lined with red tissue paper. Ask guests to dress in red and/or black.

Arrange several small tables with chairs around the party room for intimate seating. Cover the tables with red tablecloths and black lace overlays.

Use white napkins tied with black ribbon and a red rose tucked underneath. Fold small fans from black paper for place cards and use red pillar candles for centerpieces.

Decorate the buffet table with a centerpiece of red roses and black Spanish fans.

Serve traditional Spanish food, such as a variety of tapas, gazpacho, paella and flan on elegant silver trays and bowls.

Decorate the room with potted palms, strings of tiny white lights and lots of red candles. Play romantic background music.

Dance the tango or hire an instructor to teach the tango.

Give prizes in various categories for costumes and dance performances.

For favors, give chocolate roses and framed photos of the guests performing the Tango.

"Mad Hatter" Bridal Shower

Invite your guests to a bridal shower where each guest creates an unusual hat covered with shower gifts that are attached by string or wire. Assign a different household or marriage-related theme to each person, and have them decorate their hats with appropriate items. Some possibilities: kitchen, bath, garden, bedroom, sewing, romance or entertainment.

Attach the invitation to a tiny straw hat that is decorated with ribbon and silk flowers. Don't forget to tell your guests to wear their "Shower-Gift Hats". Mail the invitation inside a small tissue-lined box.

Use decorated hatboxes arranged at various heights on your serving table to hold some of your food items.

Make sugar cookies in the shape of a straw hat (adhere a 1" cookie to the center of a 3" cookie using frosting) and decorate with ribbons and flowers made with tinted frosting. Place each cookie inside a tiny hat-shaped box and give as favors. You can find small papier-maché boxes with lids at many craft stores. Simply paint them or cover them with pretty gift wrapping paper.

Provide a "modeling runway" for your guests to walk while describing their hats. This is a fun activity to video record and show during the last half hour of the party.

Give prizes for the hats in several categories: most creative, most colorful, most bizarre, etc. Take instant photos of guests in their special hats and place in small frames to give as favors.

"Always a Bridesmaid" Party

Stage a fun party where your guests wear old bridesmaid's dresses or vintage formals from a second-hand clothing store.

The invitation can be a fake, over-the-top wedding invitation attached to plastic wedding bells with a satin bow. Mail in a tissue-lined box. Be sure to tell your guests to wear their favorite or most embarrassing bridesmaid's dress— with white gloves, of course!

Cover your serving table with a white tablecloth and drape a tulle garland around the edge to resemble the cake table at a real wedding. Use silver candelabras for elegance.

Serve your treats from silver or crystal serving trays and tiered platters. All your food should be white, such as petit fours with white icing (cut them into the shape of wedding bells using a cookie cutter), mini cheesecakes and tea sandwiches. Serve drinks from champagne glasses.

Have a fashion show where each guest models her gown on a runway. Take lots of pictures and video record the event, then play it during the last half-hour of the party. Award each guest a "prize" for her costume (most outrageous, most colorful, most creative, most embarrassing, etc.).

Party favors can be tiny nosegays of real or silk white roses for your guests to carry while modeling their dresses. Simply cut the stems of each flower to about 6" long and bundle about 5 or 6 blooms together (depending on their size). Wrap the stems with florist's tape and ribbon to hold them together.

Surprise Parties

Come As You Are Party

Surprise your friends with a crack-of-dawn breakfast or a mid-night "snack-fest" when you arrive at their homes for a "come as you are" party, then whisk them away to your event.

The number of guests you include will be limited to how many people you can fit in your car or van—unless you decide to rent a small bus or have a co-conspirator collect a separate group of guests.

Video record their reactions when you show up at their doors. Play the video during the party as part of the entertainment.

Give prizes for the most surprised, most grumpy, most disheveled, etc.

Have a breakfast food buffet waiting at the party destination. Or serve a "build-your-own" pancake bar or breakfast sandwich bar.

Challenge your guests' mental faculties with the Memory game described on page 24. Or give each guest a pen and paper and ask them to write down as many words as they can in two minutes that relate to sleeping. Read some of the answers aloud for more entertainment.

For favors, give each guest an inexpensive sleep mask. Decorate each one with lace, ribbon or rhinestones, if you like.

Grandma's First
Grandbaby Shower

Surprise a grandma-to-be with
a shower to equip her with all
the items she'll need to babysit
her new grandchild.

Attach the invitation to a baby rattle and mail in a box lined
with blue and pink tissue paper. Let your guests know the
party is a surprise. Ask them to wear blue or pink—
depending on their guess for the sex of the unborn infant. If
you like, ask each guest to bring a baby photo of herself to
use in a party game.

Decorate your serving table with a blue and pink tablecloth
and napkins and include a few toys for the centerpiece.
Cover a second small table to hold the gifts.

Serve tea sandwiches filled with flavored cream cheese that
is tinted with pink or blue food coloring. Use a cookie
cutter to cut them into the shape of baby bottles or diaper
shirts. Cut petit fours into these shapes, as well, and ice
with blue or pink icing. Serve pink-colored punch.

For a fun activity, play "Baby Gift Bingo". Give each guest
a blank bingo card and ask them to fill in the squares with
items the future grandma might receive as gifts during the
party. As the gifts are opened, the guests mark off items on
their cards until someone gets a bingo. Or play the "Guess
Who" game. Pass around the infant photos that your guests
brought and let everyone guess which photo matches which
person.

For favors, give each guest a sugar cookie that is cut into
the shape of a baby bottle and decorated with blue and pink
icing. Place in a clear cellophane bag and tie closed with
blue or pink ribbon.

Surprise Location Party

Surprise your guests with a mystery location party. Your invitation will tell them the date, time and location for where the party begins, but not the final destination. It might read: "Come Prepared for a Surprising Good Time!" Be sure to tell your guests how to dress for the event, depending on its location.

Attach your invitation to an object that hints at the location, such as a fake butterfly for a butterfly exhibit, a plush parrot toy for a rainforest exhibit, a tiny plastic zebra for the zoo, a cut-out of an anchor for a boat, a bottle of sand for the beach, a baseball card for a baseball game, cotton candy for a carnival, etc. Choose an interesting location in your area that your guests might enjoy.

The number of guests you can invite will depend on the location, your budget, and your transportation capacity.

For food, you might: pack a picnic lunch or dinner for the park or zoo; provide a tailgate spread at a sporting event; grill burgers or hot dogs at the beach; or buy food for your guests at an amusement park or museum.

The entertainment will be supplied by your party location, but if the travel time is more than 15 minutes, you might provide activities during the trip, such as singing songs or answering trivia questions that relate to the destination.

Give each guest a small trinket or memento from the destination: sea shell from the beach, pennant from the game, postcard from the museum, etc.

"This is Your Life" Party

Plan a birthday party for a friend or family member where the birthday party is not the surprise. The surprise will be a presentation of "This is Your Life".

You'll need to do some sleuthing for this party. Dig up old photos of the honoree and contact old friends and family members who can supply you with interesting stories.

Tell the birthday person to arrive at a time that is later than your other guests, so he or she will be surprised by the party theme and guests. Decorate the room with enlarged photos and memorabilia from his or her past. Include items from the person's hobbies or career.

Serve some of the honoree's favorite foods. Decorate the serving table with photos of the person at various ages and items relating to his or her life.

Invite guests who can tell stories about events that occurred during the person's lifetime and how they affected others.

Play a trivia game with questions about the person's life (where they were born, where they went to school, jobs they held, hobbies, accidents or childhood illnesses like measles or chicken pox, favorite vacations, favorite foods, favorite music, favorite movies, etc.)

Play music from a period during his or her lifetime and invite guests to dance to the music if appropriate.

Video record the event for the honoree and provide copies on computer disks for other guests, as well.

Impromptu Wedding

If you and your groom don't want to deal with the hassles or expense of a large, traditional wedding, but you still want your family and close friends to attend, then stage a surprise wedding.

Invite your guests to a regular party and surprise them with a real wedding. The two of you can choose any theme you want, based on your common interests, hobbies, favorite food or music.

The number of guests you can invite will be limited because you'll probably have the event at home, but that's one advantage of hosting a surprise wedding—it keeps the guest list, and therefore the budget, in check.

Make sure you follow through with your theme, starting with a creative invitation that piques your guests' curiosity (don't even hint that there's a wedding involved), serve theme-related food that appeals to the eyes as well as the taste buds, and set the stage with decorations, lighting and music that fit your theme.

You'll need to get your marriage license and hire a clergy member to perform the ceremony, but all the other details of your wedding will be your personal choice.

Another advantage of an impromptu wedding: you won't need to negotiate family disputes about the details or compromise on any of your choices. You can choose to have some or all of the activities usually included in a traditional wedding. But don't forget to hire a photographer or videographer to record your special day.

Give each of your guests a theme-related favor to remember your event.

Never Pass Up a Chance
to Share Friendship,
Fun & Laughter

Have a Party!

Index

About the Author

Gloria Hander Lyons has channeled 30 years of training and hands-on experience in the areas of art, interior decorating, crafting and event planning into writing creative how-to books.

Her books cover a wide range of topics including decorating your home, cooking, planning weddings and tea parties, crafting and self-publishing.

She has designed original needlework and craft projects featured in magazines, such as *Better Homes and Gardens, McCall's, Country Handcrafts* and *Crafts*.

She teaches interior decorating, self-publishing and wedding planning classes at her local community college. Much to her family's delight, her kitchen is in non-stop test mode, creating recipes for new cookbooks.

Visit her website for free craft ideas, decorating and event planning tips and taste-tempting recipes at:

www.BlueSagePress.com

Other Books by Gloria Hander Lyons

- *Easy Microwave Desserts in a Mug*

- *Easy Microwave Desserts in a Mug for Kids*

- *No Rules – Just Fun Decorating*

- *Just Fun Decorating for Tweens & Teens*

- *Decorating Basics For Men Only!*

- *Ten Common Home Decorating Mistakes & How to Avoid Them*

- *If Teapots Could Talk: Fun Ideas for Tea Parties*

- *The Super-Bride's Guide for Dodging Wedding Pitfalls*

- *Designs That Sell: How To Make Your Home Show Better and Sell Faster*

- *A Taste of Lavender: Delectable Treats with an Exotic Floral Flavor*

- *Lavender Sensations: Fragrant Herbs for Home & Bath*

- *Self-Publishing on a Budget: A Do-It-All-Yourself Guide*

- *The Secret Ingredient: Tasty Recipes with an Unusual Twist*

- *Hand Over the Chocolate & No One Gets Hurt! The Chocolate-Lover's Cookbook*

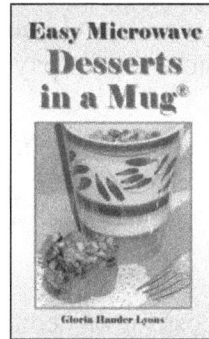

Ordering Information

To order additional copies of this book, send check or money order payable to:

Blue Sage Press
48 Borondo Pines
La Marque, TX 77568

Cost for this edition is $6.95 per book (U.S. currency only) plus $3.00 shipping and handling for the first book and $1.50 for each additional book shipped to the same U.S. address.

Texas residents add 8.25% sales tax to total order amount.

To pay by credit card or get a complete list of books written by Gloria Hander Lyons, visit our website at:

www.BlueSagePress.com.

www.ingramcontent.com/pod-product-compliance
Lightning Source LLC
Chambersburg PA
CBHW060633280326
41933CB00012B/2022